WORLD WAR I

Enzo George

Cavendish
Square

New York

Published in 2015 by Cavendish Square Publishing, LLC
243 5th Avenue, Suite 136, New York, NY 10016

© 2015 Brown Bear Books Ltd

First edition

Website: cavendishsq.com

CPSIA compliance information: Batch #WW15CSQ.

All websites were available and accurate when this book was sent to press.

Library of Congress Cataloging-in-Publication Data

George, Enzo.
World War I / Enzo George.
     pages cm. — (Primary sources in U.S.history)
Includes index.
ISBN 978-1-50260-252-7 (hardcover) ISBN 978-1-50260-261-9 (ebook)
1. World War, 1914-1918—History—Juvenile literature. I. Title.

D522.7.G45 2015b
940.4—dc23

                    2014026756

For Brown Bear Books Ltd:
Editorial Director: Lindsey Lowe
Managing Editor: Tim Cooke
Children's Publisher: Anne O'Daly
Design Manager: Keith Davis
Designer: Lynne Lennon
Picture Manager: Sophie Mortimer

Manufactured in the United States of America

CONTENTS

INTRODUCTION

Primary sources are the best way to get close to people from the past. They include the things people wrote in diaries, letters, or books; the paintings, drawings, maps, or cartoons they created; and even the buildings they constructed, the clothes they wore, or the possessions they owned. Such sources often reveal a lot about how people saw themselves and how they thought about their world.

This book collects a range of primary sources from World War I, from its outbreak in Europe in 1914 to the reaction to the U.S. decision to enter the conflict in 1917, the effect on the home front, and the impact of American troops on the fighting.

The war began with a seemingly minor incident that triggered a series of declarations of war and alliances that drew most of Europe into the conflict by the middle of 1915. The Allies—led by Britain, France, and Russia—fought the Central Powers, dominated by Germany and Austria-Hungary. A German advance on Paris was stopped, and the two sides dug into trenches that stretched through northwest France and Belgium. German submarine attacks on U.S. shipping eventually convinced the U.S. government to declare war in April 1917. U.S. troops began to influence the fighting the following year, when a final Allied offensive forced Germany to surrender.

HOW TO USE THIS BOOK

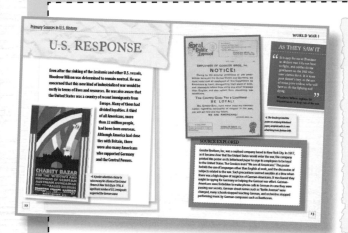

Each spread contains at least one primary source. Look out for "Source Explored" boxes that explain images from World War I and who made them and why. There are also "As They Saw It" boxes that contain quotes from people of the period.

Some boxes contain more detailed information about a particular aspect of a subject. The subjects are arranged in roughly chronological order. They focus on key events or people. There is a full timeline of the period at the back of the book.

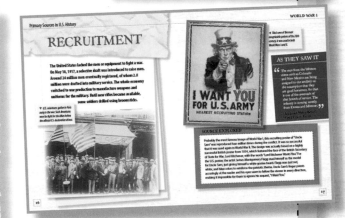

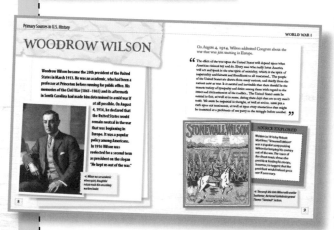

Some spreads feature a longer extract from a contemporary eyewitness. Look for the colored introduction that explains who the writer is and the origin of his or her account. These accounts are often accompanied by a related visual primary source.

OUTBREAK OF WAR

On June 28, 1914, Archduke Franz Ferdinand, the heir to the Austrian throne, was assassinated by a Serbian terrorist. That triggered a series of alliances that drew much of Europe into the conflict. The Axis powers—Germany, Austria-Hungary, the Ottoman Empire, and their allies—fought the Allies, who were Britain, France, Russia, Italy, and their allies. War spread to Europe's colonies around the world.

▼ *Austrians celebrate the start of the war in Vienna. Most Europeans believed the conflict would be very short.*

▼ *The* Daily Chronicle *reports the assassination of Franz Ferdinand and his wife, Sophie.*

Daily

NO. 4,438. LONDON, MONDAY, JUNE 29

HEIR TO USTRIAN THRONE MURDERED.

RCHDUKE AND HIS WIFE SHOT DEAD IN THE STREET.

ETERMINED PLOT.

OMB FIRST THROWN AT THEIR CAR.

ECOND ATTEMPT WITHIN AN HOUR.

BOY ASSASSIN.

MURDERED ARCHDUKE AND HIS WIFE.
The Archduke Francis Ferdinand and his wife, who was also assassinated.

the burgomaster and the members of the town council, and it was clear to all that he was then in a furious temper, and bitterly resentful of what had happened.
The burgomaster stepped forward to

19-YEAR-OLD ASSASSIN.

MANY PERSONS INJURED BY THE FIRST BOMB.

SOURCE EXPLORED

The London *Daily Chronicle* of June 29, 1914 reports the killing of Franz Ferdinand and his wife, Sophie. The killers were Serbs seeking independence from the Austro-Hungarian Empire. The Austrians declared war on Serbia on July 28. In return, Serbia's ally, Russia, went to war with Austria-Hungary. This drew in Austria's ally, Germany, which declared war on Russia on August 1. Germany then declared war on France, because the German war plan relied upon defeating France before facing Russia, in order to avoid fighting on two fronts. Germany's offensive against France involved German troops invading Belgium, but that country's neutrality had been guaranteed by Britain. On August 4, 1914, therefore, Britain and its empire joined the war. Countries such as Italy and the Ottoman Empire also eventually joined the conflict.

WOODROW WILSON

Woodrow Wilson became the twenty-eighth president of the United States in March 1913. He was an academic, who had been a professor at Princeton before running for public office. His memories of the Civil War (1861–1865) and its aftermath had made him determined to avoid war if at all possible. On August 4, 1914, he declared that the United States would remain neutral in the war that was beginning in Europe. It was a popular policy among Americans. In 1916 Wilson was reelected for a second term as president on the slogan "He kept us out of the war."

◀ Wilson was an academic whose quiet, thoughtful nature made him an unlikely wartime leader.

On August 4, 1914, Wilson addressed Congress about the war that was just starting in Europe:

> The effect of the war upon the United States will depend upon what American citizens say and do. Every man who really loves America will act and speak in the true spirit of neutrality, which is the spirit of impartiality and fairness and friendliness to all concerned... The people of the United States are drawn from many nations, and chiefly from the nations now at war. It is natural and inevitable that there should be the utmost variety of sympathy and desire among them with regard to the issues and circumstances of the conflict... The United States must be neutral in fact, as well as in name, during these days that are to try men's souls. We must be impartial in thought, as well as action, must put a curb upon our sentiments, as well as upon every transaction that might be construed as a preference of one party to the struggle before another.

SOURCE EXPLORED

Written in 1916 by Robert Mortimer, "Stonewall Wilson" was a popular song praising Wilson for keeping his country out of the war. The cover of the sheet music shows the president leading his troops, however, to suggest that the president would indeed go to war if necessary.

◀ The song's title links Wilson with another Southerner, the famed Confederate general Thomas "Stonewall" Jackson.

SINKING OF THE *LUSITANIA*

The U.S. policy of neutrality was difficult to maintain. German U-boats, or submarines, attacked U.S. vessels heading to Britain. The Germans ignored Wilson's protests that such ships were neutral. In May 1915, a U-boat sank the passenger ship *Lusitania*, with a heavy loss of life. Wilson got Germany to agree to stop attacking passenger ships. For the time being, he had kept America out of the war.

▼ *The 1,198 people who lost their lives when the* Lusitania *was sunk included 128 Americans sailing to Europe.*

Chrissie Aitken from Scotland was a passenger on the *Lusitania*. She recalls the moment the ship sank:

" We were all sitting at lunch, and as a girl friend was waiting for me I left the table before the others, and I never saw them again. I was in my cabin when the torpedo struck, and it seemed to hit a part of the boat near me. Instinctively I seemed to know we had been torpedoed, for it had been in all our minds right across the whole way, though it was treated mostly as a joke. We thought we got safely so far, all possible danger was past, but we made a terrible mistake. The smoke was already coming into my cabin, and I rushed above. A great many people were running about, but others took it very quietly though they were lowering the boats. It was everybody for themselves. "

▲ This illustration of a woman and her baby sinking in the dark sea was one of the most haunting posters of the war.

SOURCE EXPLORED

After the sinking of the *Lusitania*, the artist Fred Spear painted this poster of a drowning mother and baby for the Boston Committee of Public Safety in 1915. Although it was a powerful image, it did not mean much without any mention of the *Lusitania*. Eventually it was withdrawn because it was considered too depressing.

U.S. RESPONSE

Even after the sinking of the *Lusitania* and other U.S. vessels, Woodrow Wilson was determined to remain neutral. He was concerned that this new kind of industrialized war would be costly in terms of lives and resources. He was also aware that the United States was a country of recent immigrants from Europe. Many of them had divided loyalties. A third of all Americans, more than thirty-two million people, had been born overseas. Although America had close ties with Britain, there were also many Americans who supported Germany and the Central Powers.

◀ *A poster advertises a bazaar to raise money for citizens of the Central Powers in New York City in 1916. A significant number of U.S. immigrants supported the German cause.*

REFERENCES:
CHEMICAL NATIONAL BANK
THE CHATHAM AND PHOENIX NATIONAL BANK
BROADWAY AT 33th STREET
COLONIAL BANK
116th STREET AND COLUMBUS AVENUE

GOSSLER BROS., Inc.
903-905 COLUMBUS AVENUE, NEW YORK

NEW YORK,_____191_

EMPLOYEES OF GOSSLER BROS., Inc.
NOTICE!

Owing to the peculiar conditions of war possi-
bilities between the United States and Germany, we
must insist that all employees of this Corporation be
Americans by heart, disregarding their place of birth,
and absolutely refrain from using any other language
than English, and also refrain from discussing war
conditions.

This Country Gives You a Livelihood—
BE LOYAL!

We, Gossler Bros., have never used any discrimi-
nation regarding nationality or religion in the past,
nor will we now and the future.
WE ARE AMERICANS!

GOSSLER BROS., Inc.

A GOOD RULE!
WE HAVE THE REPUTATION FOR SERVING
THE BEST MERCHANDISE AT A PRICE AS
REASONABLE AS PRACTICAL BUSINESS
METHODS PERMIT.

GOSSLER BROS. INC.
"SEAFOOD FRESH FROM OCEAN DEPTHS"

AS THEY SAW IT

" It is easy for me as President
to declare war. I do not have
to fight, and neither do the
gentlemen on the Hill who
now clamor for it. It is some
poor farmer's boy, or the son
of some poor widow, who will
have to do the fighting and
dying. "

—Woodrow Wilson explains his
determination to keep out of the war.

◄ *The Gosslers printed the
poster on company letterhead
paper, complete with its own
advertising texts (bottom left).*

SOURCE EXPLORED

Gossler Brothers, Inc, was a seafood company based in New York City. In 1917,
as it became clear that the United States would enter the war, the company
printed this poster on its letterhead paper to urge its employees to be loyal to
the United States. The Gosslers insist "We are Americans." The poster forbids
the use of languages other than English at work and the discussion of subjects
related to the war. Such precautions seemed sensible at a time when there
was a high degree of suspicion of German Americans. It was feared they might
be spying for Germany or helping the German war effort. German Americans
were forbidden to make phone calls in German in case they were passing war
secrets. German street names such as "Berlin Avenue" were changed, many
schools stopped teaching German, and orchestras stopped performing music
by German composers such as Beethoven.

U.S. DECLARATION OF WAR

▶ *This colored photograph shows Woodrow Wilson asking Congress to declare war on Germany on April 2, 1917.*

On April 6, 1917, the United States declared war on Germany. Wilson had realized that U.S. involvement was inevitable, despite his reluctance. Germany had continued to sink U.S. ships. In addition, the Germans had sent a secret telegram to Mexico, offering U.S. territory in return for Mexican support in the war. Wilson also saw that taking part in the war would give the United States a key role in the reshaping of Europe once the war was over.

SOURCE EXPLORED

On the night the United States declared war on Germany, the vaudeville star Nora Bayes sang a new song called "Over There." Its message that "the Yanks are coming" was highly popular. The song had only been written that morning by the Broadway composer and performer George M. Cohan. He had started to hum the tune at breakfast and had written the words by the time he reached his office. "Over There" went on to become the most popular song of the war in the United States, selling over two million copies.

AS THEY SAW IT

" Over there, over there
Send the word, send the word, over there
That the Yanks are coming, the Yanks are coming
The drum tum-tumming everywhere
So prepare, say a pray'r
Send the word, send the word, to beware
We'll be over, we're coming over
And we won't be back 'til it's over, over there. "

–Chorus from "Over There," George M. Cohan, April 6, 1917

◀ The music for "Over There" was illustrated by an image of the song's first singer, Norah Bayes. She is wearing a uniform resembling something from the American Revolution.

RECRUITMENT

The United States lacked the men or equipment to fight a war. On May 18, 1917, a selective draft was introduced to raise men. Around twenty-four million men eventually registered, of whom 2.8 million were drafted into military service. The economy switched to war production to manufacture weapons and uniforms for the military. Until new rifles became available, some soldiers drilled using broomsticks.

▼ U.S. volunteers gather in Paris early in the war. Such Americans went to fight for the Allies before the official U.S. declaration of war.

I WANT YOU
FOR U.S. ARMY
NEAREST RECRUITING STATION

◀ *This is one of the most recognizable posters of the twentieth century. It was used in both World Wars I and II.*

AS THEY SAW IT

❝ The men from the Western states such as Colorado and New Mexico are being assigned to the artillery on the assumption that they are good horsemen, for that is one of the essentials of that branch of service. The infantry is coming mostly from Kansas and Missouri. ❞

–Lieutenant Milton Bernet, Camp Fuston, Kansas.

SOURCE EXPLORED

Probably the most famous image of World War I, this recruiting poster of "Uncle Sam" was reproduced four million times during the conflict. It was so successful that it was used again in World War II. The design was actually based on a highly successful British poster from 1914, which featured the face of the British Secretary of State for War, Lord Kitchener, with the words "Lord Kitchener Wants You." For the U.S. poster, the artist James Montgomery Flagg used himself as the model for Uncle Sam, just giving himself a white goatee beard. Flagg uses just red, white, and blue colors to reinforce the patriotic theme. Uncle Sam's finger points accusingly at the reader and his eyes seem to follow the viewer in every direction, making it impossible for them to ignore his request, "I Want You."

THE WAR IN EUROPE

▲ *This artist's impression shows German troops at night looking out from their trench at "no-man's land."*

In Europe, the war had reached a stalemate. After the German advance of 1914 through Belgium into France became bogged down, the two sides had dug a series of trenches that now faced each other for 400 miles (640 km), from the English Channel to Switzerland. The armies attacked each other across the narrow strip of "no-man's land" that separated the opposing trenches. Battles were fought with great loss of life for very little territorial gain. Captured territory was soon lost again.

▲ *This image is taken from a movie that included genuine scenes from the Somme combined with staged incidents.*

This photograph seems to show British soldiers leaving their trenches, or going "over the top," on the first day of the Battle of the Somme on July 1, 1916. In fact, it is a photo from a movie about the battle. This scene was staged behind the lines, because the actual attack was too dangerous for a cameraman. The British Army lost some 20,000 dead on the bloodiest day in its history. The Somme is still seen as an example of the huge waste of life caused by unimaginative tactics. In fact, commanders on both sides tried to work out the best way to capture positions defended by weapons such as machine guns. Offensives such as the Somme often resulted in stalemate and cost thousands of lives.

WESTERN FRONT

The Western Front was dominated by the trench systems that both sides dug. The frontline trenches were often very close together, defended by barbed wire and minefields. Communications trenches led back to safer areas. Batteries of heavy artillery rained shells down on enemy lines, turning the landscape into a sea of mud with no vegetation.

THE DOUGHBOYS

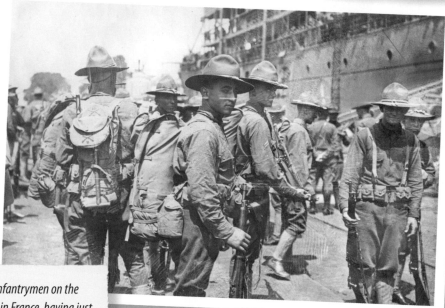

▲ U.S. infantrymen on the quayside in France, having just disembarked from their ship.

The American Expeditionary Force (AEF) started to arrive in Europe in June 1917. The "Doughboys" took their nickname from the nineteenth century, although no one knows its origins. The AEF commander, General John "Black Jack" Pershing, had strong views about his small army. He was determined to take time to train his troops in France. He wanted them to get used to trench warfare. He also refused to put the Doughboys under Allied command. It was not until the middle of 1918 that U.S. troops began to join the battle in any great numbers.

Private Malcolm D. Aitken, 5th Marines, 2nd Division, recalled his journey to the front lines:

" Camion [truck] travel at first, rain, mud, bombings, and transport of every shape and kind, including men, going in or coming out; the center of the road was open for Command [vehicles], Ambulances... Dark as black as you want to call it. No lights except on vehicles, no smoking in the ranks, no food, no rest. Just slosh along keeping in touch with [the] man ahead, with your outstretched fingers. After falling in the slippery, slidy, water-filled side road area [a large ditch]. After much time like this we lined out across an area among some small trees, shrubs, and grassy stuff. **"**

The Doughboys Make Good

SOURCE EXPLORED

This illustration by Edward Penfield appeared on the cover of *Collier's* magazine on August 10, 1918. By then, U.S. forces were turning the tide of war in the Allies' favor. The image shows two Doughboys manning a machine gun. It sums up the huge difference U.S. forces made to the Allies, not just in terms of manpower, but also in resupplying the Allies' supplies of weapons and hardware, which were running low.

▲ *The slogan on this magazine cover reflects the positive effect the arrival of U.S. troops had on the Allied war effort.*

WAR IN THE TRENCHES

Life in the trenches was a routine of mud, rats, and being cold, wet, and hungry. The trenches filled with rain and many soldiers developed trench foot, a painful skin infection. German trenches were often better built than those of the Allies. When a bombardment signaled an enemy attack, troops took shelter until the artillery barrage ended, then took up their firing positions.

▼ U.S. soldiers keep their heads down during an artillery bombardment near Toul, France, on March 22, 1918.

SOURCE EXPLORED

This photograph shows U.S. officers enjoying a meal in a trench that looks very solidly built. By 1917, the Allies had improved their trench-building techniques. This trench is dry and has furniture. Heavy beams help reinforce the walls in case of artillery attack.

▲ U.S. officers enjoy a meal in their trench during a lull in the fighting on the Western Front.

British fusilier Guy Chapman recalls how he and his fellow soldiers built a defensive parapet, or wall, overnight to reinforce part of a trench:

" The trench was not a trench at all. The bottom may have been two feet below ground level. An enormous breastwork rose in the darkness some ten or more feet high. All about was an air of bustle. Men came and went... Men were lifting filled sandbags on to the parapet and beating them into the wall with shovels. Bullets cracked in the darkness...

As the night passed, the labour grew less and less tumultuous. Men came in over the parapet, settled down in the corners of firebays and dropped asleep... Here and there a man boiled up a can of tea... I lay down and blew out the light. Mysterious rustlings became audible... Rats, I guessed, and shuddered. "

THE AIR WAR

World War I broke out just eleven years after the Wright Brothers' first airplane flight. Both sides soon began to make use of the new technology. The first airplanes were used for reconnaissance, but by the time U.S. troops arrived in Europe, planes were being used as fighters and bombers. Fighter pilots, known as aces, clashed in "dogfights" high above the trenches. The war's leading ace was the German Baron Manfred von Richthofen, with eighty confirmed "kills" of enemy aircraft.

▼ *The leading U.S. ace was Captain Eddie Rickenbacker, who shot down twenty-six enemy airplanes in his Spad XIII biplane.*

◀ Searchlights illuminate the long, menacing shape of a Zeppelin in the night sky above London.

SOURCE EXPLORED

Searchlights pick out a cigar-shaped airship in the sky above London. The German airships, known as Zepplins for their inventor, first appeared in spring 1915. Londoners feared they would launch a bombing campaign against the city. In fact, the invention of incendiary bullets, that set the airships on fire, made Zeppelins too risky to fly.

Eddie Rickenbacker remembers his first combat against a German pilot flying a **Pfalz** fighter. Tracer bullets give out light to help pilots see the direction they are firing:

❝ Every fourth shell was a tracer, and I could see two streaks of fire pouring into the **Pfalz**'s tail assembly. I held the triggers down and pulled back on the stick slightly, lifting the nose of the plane. It was like raising a garden hose. I could see the stream of fire climbing up the fuselage and into the pilot's seat.

The plane swerved. It was no longer being flown. I pulled out of the dive and watched the **Pfalz** curve down and crash. I had brought down my first enemy airplane. ❞

THE WAR AT SEA

▲ In this postcard, German submarines approach an enemy coast. The U-boats sank 5,554 Allied and neutral vessels during the war.

In the decade before World War I, Britain and Germany raced to build powerful battleships. However, once the war began, the battleships only fought each other once, at the Battle of Jutland in summer 1916. Instead, the Germans used submarines, or U-boats, to attack Allied and neutral shipping in the hope of starving Britain into surrender. The Allies responded by organizing merchant ships into convoys protected by warships, which reduced losses. The U-boat threat lessened further when the United States joined the war, making more warships available to guard the convoys.

◀ *Hans Rudi Erdt was a German artist. He showed the U-boat commanders as being heroic figures. In contrast, the Allies viewed them almost as war criminals.*

AS THEY SAW IT

" We were soon amid the rushing of turbulent water that is caused by a sub directly after submerging. We let go [a depth charge] set to explode at about 80 feet deep...
We were soon rewarded by seeing the color of the water turn black in the immediate vicinity of the explosion. "

—Seaman William Duke, Jr., recalls destroying a U-boat.

SOURCE EXPLORED

This German poster features a large "U" as part of the phrase "U Boote Heraus!" ("The U-Boats Are Out!") The poster was created by Hans Rudi Erdt to promote a movie that was made in 1917 to show the German people their navy's remarkable new weapon. A U-boat commander uses a periscope to check the surface of the ocean, while a cargo ship sinks after being struck by a torpedo. The poster presents the commander as a heroic figure, using new technology to strike at Germany's enemies. In fact, submarines were controversial because they sank neutral vessels. In addition, most U-boat attacks were made on the surface. The vessels could only stay underwater for brief periods of time.

AFRICAN AMERICANS AT WAR

Many of the 370,000 African Americans who served in the military saw the war as a chance to show their loyalty and improve their civil rights at home. Most of the 200,000 who served overseas were only in service roles, although 40,000 were in combat divisions. The U.S. Army was segregated on racial lines, and African Americans faced prejudice from white soldiers.

▼ *African American infantrymen advance in northwest France in November 1918, during the Meuse–Argonne Offensive.*

SOURCE EXPLORED

The Committee on Public Information commissioned this poster to celebrate the achievements of the African American 369th Infantry Regiment, also known as the Harlem Hellfighters. Charles Gustrine of Chicago was the artist. He showed the all-black unit from New York under the watchful eye of President Abraham Lincoln, who originally freed the slaves. Above Lincoln's signature is a quote from his Gettysburg Address that directly links the bravery of the African American soldiers with the struggle of the Union to preserve freedom and liberty. The Hellfighters were the first American unit to fight the Germans and they served the longest at the front—191 days—of any U.S. unit. The French awarded 171 members of the unit the *Croix de Guerre*, a medal for bravery.

▲ Abraham Lincoln looks on as Germans surrender to the Harlem Hellfighters in Charles Gustrine's poster.

AS THEY SAW IT

" My dear Sister,
Your letter received and always glad to hear from you. I can't say that I like the Army life, it is a hard life to live and they are so mean to the colored boys here. They curse and beat them just like they were dogs and a fellow can't even get sick. Oh! It is an awfully mean place. I will be so glad when they send me away from here. "

—African American Private Stanley Moore writes to his sister from Camp Travis, Texas, 1917.

LIFE ON THE HOME FRONT

All Americans played their part in the war effort. Every citizen was made responsible for supporting their soldiers in Europe by conserving food, gas, and electricity. In 1917, President Wilson created the U.S. Food Administration to oversee food and fuel control, under the leadership of Herbert Hoover. Hoover used a campaign of posters to help cut domestic food consumption by 15 percent during the course of the war.

JOIN THE UNITED-STATES SCHOOL GARDEN ARMY

ENLIST NOW

Write to The United States School Garden Army, Bureau of Education, Department of Interior, Washington, D.C.

◀ This poster encouraged U.S. schools to use their land for the creation of gardens so they could grow vegetables for food.

Little AMERICANS
Do your bit

Eat Oatmeal-Corn meal mush-
Hominy - other corn cereals -
and Rice with milk.
Save the wheat for our soldiers.

Leave nothing on your plate

UNITED STATES FOOD ADMINISTRATION

"HOOVERIZING"

During World War I, Herbert Hoover, later the thirty-first U.S. President, had the important job of U.S. Food Administrator. He introduced a voluntary program of conservation of food, gas, and other essentials. The effort was so successful and widespread that Americans nicknamed the conservation effort "hooverizing."

◀ *This poster was created by the celebrated illustrator Cushman Parker, who often included children in the advertisements he painted for publication in popular magazines.*

SOURCE EXPLORED

Nobody was exempt from the drive to save food. This propaganda poster from 1917 is addressed to "young Americans," who are told to eat up all their food. "Food Will Win the War" was a popular slogan, and mothers were encouraged to get their families to avoid meat on Mondays and wheat products on Wednesdays. Wheat was easier to transport to Europe than cornmeal, which spoiled on the voyage. Voluntary food conservation helped to prevent compulsory rationing and helped to feed the army at home and in Europe. There was even enough spare food to feed Allied forces. After the war, the extra food sent to Europe stopped Europeans from starving.

WOMEN AT WAR

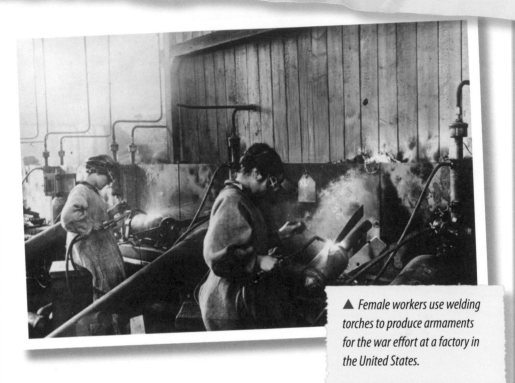

▲ Female workers use welding torches to produce armaments for the war effort at a factory in the United States.

At the start of World War I in 1914, the United States had the richest and most industrialized economy in the world. After the draft was introduced in 1917, almost five million men went to serve in the military, leaving essential jobs vacant. The government encouraged women to fill these roles. Women worked in factories, in offices, on railroads, and on farms. Many African Americans also moved from the South to the North to take up jobs left by men going to war.

◀ This poster was designed by Ernest Hamlin Baker. It shows women marching off to work wearing clothes for particular jobs.

SOURCE EXPLORED

This poster for the Young Women's Christian Association encouraged women to take up war work. For the women, the chance to work was also the first time they had experienced economic freedom. Some did not like it after the war, when returning soldiers took back their jobs. Women said their war service showed that they were worthy of having the right to vote. They received this right in 1920.

An airplane dropped thousands of cards on a crowd gathered at Seaside Park, Bridgeport, Connecticut, on September 21, 1918. They read:

❝ How easy it is for me to drop this message to you! And one of the Kaiser's airmen could just as easily drop a bomb, and he would in a minute if he could. The Kaiser [German leader] doesn't care who he hits, old or young—women or children—they are all alike to him. That's the kind of man we are fighting.

Why don't you women retaliate? You can fight at the front and live home by enlisting for pleasant easy work in the nearest munition factory. Gen. Pershing wants more men, so Uncle Sam says to you 'Making munitions is a woman's job—will you go to work today and hasten the end of this terrible struggle?' ❞

PAYING FOR THE WAR

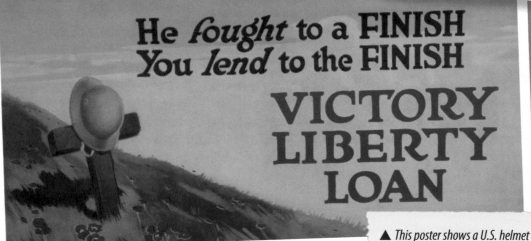

He *fought* to a FINISH
You *lend* to the FINISH

VICTORY LIBERTY LOAN

▲ *This poster shows a U.S. helmet on a grave on a hillside of poppies. It urges Americans to buy Liberty Loans to pay for the war.*

Despite its wealth, even the United States had to raise money to pay for World War I. It imposed a series of taxes on income, alcohol, tobacco, and other goods. The government also sold bonds, a type of savings certificate, which citizens bought in return for the promise of the bond being repaid with interest in the future. "Liberty" bonds (later called "Victory" bonds) were sold to raise money, and poster campaigns tried to convince Americans that it was their patriotic duty to buy them.

Don't dream of Victory—

FIGHT FOR IT!
Buy Liberty Bonds

◄ *The United Cigar Stores Company sponsored the production of this poster—in return for the publicity it gave their business.*

FOUR-MINUTE MEN

The message to buy war bonds was repeated often by the four-minute men. These volunteers gave brief speeches—lasting four minutes—on a range of topics to do with the war, from buying war bonds to the need to look out for enemy spies. To reach the biggest audience, the talks were broadcast in movie theaters between reel changes.

SOURCE EXPLORED

There were four issues of Liberty Bonds between April 1917 and September 1918. This poster uses two fighting men and a female figure labeled "Victory"—who looks a little like the Statue of Liberty—to encourage Americans to buy bonds. The first Liberty Bond sale did not meet with much public enthusiasm. To make later bond sales more attractive, the government enlisted movie stars such as Charlie Chaplin and Mary Pickford to urge the public to buy. Businesses such as the United Cigar Stores Company featured in this 1917 poster were eager to publicize the bonds because they were a form of advertising as well as a means of raising money for the war.

FIRST U.S. BATTLES

The first battle to involve U.S. troops took place on May 28, 1918. The 1st Division, the most experienced in the U.S. Army, captured Cantigny on the Somme in northern France. Within a month, troops of the U.S. 2nd and 3rd Divisions also cleared Belleau Wood. The Germans counterattacked in July but were defeated at Chateau-Thierry, just 60 miles (96 km) from Paris.

▼ *U.S. troops leave their trenches and go "over the top" for the first time at Cantigny on May 28, 1918.*

The French artist Lucien Jonas drew this picture of a U.S. Marine strangling a German during the Battle of Belleau Wood. Dense foliage made fighting difficult, and the Marines and German soldiers engaged in heavy hand-to-hand fighting. The American has pushed the German against a shattered tree stump. Many of the trees in the wood were felled by artillery fire.

◀ Lucien Jonas shows a desperate hand-to-hand fight as a U.S. Marine pushes a German soldier onto the stump of a tree shattered by artillery fire.

Lieutenant Phelps Harding of the 306th Infantry Regiment wrote home from France on September 10, 1918:

" My orders took me first to Chateau Thierry. You have probably read about the fighting in that city. The place is pretty badly banged up from shell fire but not as badly as most of the smaller villages beyond it. The Huns [Germans] tore things up in great shape—statues, ornaments, and pictures in homes were broken and cut up as if by a band of plundering outlaws.

From Chateau Thierry my trail led toward the Ourcq River, which our men had to cross under heavy machine-gun fire and artillery shelling. Beyond was open country. You will see what a tough proposition it was when you read the casualty list for the few days when the Boche [Germans] were retreating... "

ST. MIHIEL

▲ U.S. troops fire a huge artillery gun at German lines. The gun was so large and heavy it had to be moved by railroad.

On September 12, 1918, seven U.S. and two French divisions attacked German troops occupying a salient, or bulge, in Allied lines at St. Mihiel. After a four-hour artillery bombardment, some 500,000 U.S. troops overcame a smaller-sized German force. Although the offensive ran out of steam, and the Germans had already begun to evacuate the area in any case, the first major U.S.-led operation of the war was seen as a major success and helped to raise Allied morale.

SOURCE EXPLORED

This poster was painted by the French artist Maurice Toussaint and used by French Railways to promote St. Mihiel as a destination in 1919, after the end of the war. The painting shows an American soldier sitting on what seems to be the wreckage of some military hardware—possibly a tank—on top of a hill overlooking a river flowing through a town in the valley. The scene is peaceful. Golden sunlight illuminates the soldier, which makes him seem more heroic. The sunlight also suggests not only the promise of the U.S.-led victory of March 1918 but also the bright future that awaits France after the defeat of Germany. In reality, the French countryside and towns along the Western Front were left in ruins after nearly five years of fighting.

▲ *In the light of a new day, an American soldier looks out over the town of St. Mihiel in its peaceful valley.*

AS THEY SAW IT

66 For four hours the deafening roar continued as our messengers of death were hurled into enemy territory. Then at 5:00 our infantry preceded by tanks went over the top, making a picture of dash and activity. Not content with ordinary progress the boys of our division leaped ahead of the clumsy tanks and pressed forward in irresistible waves to the German trenches. 99

—Corporal Elmer Sherwood describes the St. Mihiel offensive.

DEFEAT OF GERMANY

The Meuse-Argonne Offensive led by the American Expeditionary Force (AEF) began on September 26, 1918, in the Argonne Forest in northwest France. It was part of a general Allied push known as the Hundred Days Offensive. Stretched along a 44-mile (71-km) front, the offensive was the largest in U.S. military history. Some 1.2 million U.S. soldiers were involved, of whom 26,000 were killed. After forty-seven days of fighting, the Americans cleared the forest and were advancing when news came of the armistice.

◄ *Thousands of German troops began to surrender during the final Allied offensives in France in early fall 1918.*

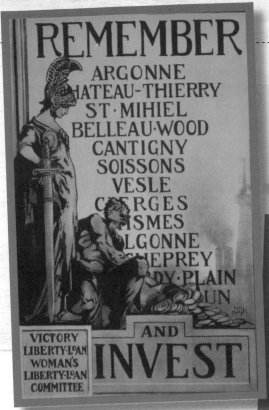

◀ In this 1917 poster a
figure presents a sack of coins
to a sword-carrying woman
wearing a warrior's helmet.

SOURCE EXPLORED

This 1917 poster produced
by the Women's Liberty Loan
Committee uses a list of AEF
engagements in the war to
urge Americans to take out
more Liberty Loans. It uses
the kind of lettering and
figures used on tombstones
and memorials. The names
of the battles would have
been familiar to Americans
following the progress of the
war in Europe.

Ernest Peixotto was an official war
artist with the AEF whose job was to
record the war through drawings. He
recalls watching an AEF advance:

" As the day wore on and the Bois de
Malancourt was cleaned up, I could see...
our troops emerge from the woods and start across
the open to attack the Bois de Montfaucon beyond.
Little khaki-colored toys they looked like, scattered
out in open formation...

And then a thrill went up my spine as I saw the tanks
come out, strange lumbering creatures, crawling one
after another, Indian file, rocking like ships in a heavy
sea... Shells with lurid, saffron-colored smoke—the new
antitank explosive—began to burst over them... "

VICTORY AND PEACE

Facing defeat, Germany asked for an armistice. At 11:00 a.m. on November 11, 1918, the guns stopped firing on the Western Front. A peace conference in Paris in 1919 imposed harsh terms on Germany, causing resentment that finally led to World War II in 1939. Meanwhile, Woodrow Wilson's creation of the League of Nations, a body to resolve international disputes peacefully, was weakened when the U.S. Congress failed to support it.

▼ *French and American service personnel celebrate the Armistice on November 11, 1918 in Paris, France.*

SOURCE EXPLORED

This cartoon by U.S. artist William A. Rogers shows the French general Ferdinand Foch presenting peace terms to a German officer, watched by a scruffy German eagle. The French insisted that the Germans should pay for the whole cost of the war, payments known as reparations. President Woodrow Wilson argued for a "just peace." He warned that such a harsh settlement would weaken the German economy and cause social unrest, but the British backed the French. German resentment of the Versailles Treaty was a major cause of the rise of Adolf Hitler and the Nazi Party.

▲ The cartoonist William A. Rogers takes a humorous view of France's determination to punish Germany for the war.

AS THEY SAW IT

❝ People cease chattering and there is only the sound of occasional coughing and the dry rustle of programs... There is then an absolute hush, followed by a sharp military order... And then, isolated and pitiable, come the two German delegates, Dr. Muller and Dr. Bell. The silence is terrifying... ❞

—British diplomat Harold Nicholson on the signing of the Treaty of Versailles.

TIMELINE

1914

June 28: *Archduke Franz Ferdinand of Austria is assassinated by Serbs in Sarajevo, Bosnia.*

July 28: *Austria declares war on Serbia.*

August 1: *Germany declares war on Russia.*

August 3: *Germany declares war on France.*

August 4: *The United States declares its neutrality. Britain enters the war.*

September 6: *The German advance on Paris is halted in the Battle of the Marne.*

October 18: *First Battle of Ypres.*

November 22: *Trenches now stretch along the whole of the Western Front.*

1915

February 18: *German U-boats begin to attack all vessels heading for Britain.*

April 22: *Poisonous gas is used in the trenches for the first time at the Second Battle of Ypres.*

April 27: *The Allies land at Gallipoli in Turkey in a failed attempt to knock Turkey out of the war.*

May 7: *A German U-boat sinks the liner* Lusitania, *with great loss of civilian life.*

May 31: *The Germans launch the first Zeppelin raid on London.*

September 25: *Battle of Loos begins.*

December 20: *Allied troops are evacuated from Gallipoli.*

1916

January 24: *The British introduce conscription.*

February 21: *The Battle of Verdun begins; it will last over ten months as the French defend a crucial strongpoint.*

May 31–June 1: *The Battle of Jutland. The German High Seas Fleet is forced into port for the rest of the war.*

July 1: *British troops begin the Battle of the Somme.*

August 28: *Italy declares war on Germany.*

September 2: *The British Royal Flying Corps shoots down the first Zeppelin over Britain.*

September 15: *Tanks are used for the first time in the Battle of Flers-Courcelette.*

December 18: *End of the Battle of Verdun.*

1917

January 31: *Germany says it will continue unrestricted submarine warfare.*

February 3: *The United States cuts off diplomatic relations with Germany in response to the threat of submarine attacks.*

March 15: *A communist revolution in Russia ends fighting on the Eastern Front.*

April 6: *The United States declares war on Germany and begins to mobilize troops.*

April 9: *The Battle of the Aisne begins.*

June 25: *The first U.S. troops arrive in France.*

July 31: *The Third Battle of Ypres begins.*

October 26: *The battlefield is churned into a sea of mud at the Second Battle of Passchendaele.*

November 20: *Battle of Cambrai.*

1918

March: *Germany begins its "Spring Offensive" and smashes through Allied lines.*

April 5: *The Spring Offensive comes to an end.*

May 28: *U.S. troops go into action for the first time at the Battle of Cantigny.*

June 1: *U.S. troops begin the Battle of Belleau Wood.*

August 8: *The Second Battle of Amiens introduces movement to the Western Front, as the trench lines are broken.*

September 12: *U.S. troops lauch an attack on the German salient at St. Mihiel.*

September 26: *The American Expeditionary Force begins the successful Meuse-Argonne Offensive.*

October 4: *Germany and Austria-Hungary send peace proposals to Woodrow Wilson, requesting an armistice.*

November 8: *Armistice talks begin.*

November 11: *The Armistice comes into effect at 11:00 a.m.*

1919

January 18: *The Paris Peace Conference begins.*

June 28: *The Treaty of Versailles is signed.*

GLOSSARY

alliances Formal relationships between countries that share common aims.

armistice A break in fighting arranged so that peace negotiations can be held.

artillery Large weapons such as cannons and mortars.

assassinate To murder someone because of his or her political position.

biplane An airplane with two sets of wings.

bombardment A continuous attack with bombs or shells.

bunker A fortified room that is usually underground or partly beneath the ground.

convoy A group of ships or vehicles traveling together for safety.

depth charge A bomb designed to explode at a certain depth underwater.

diplomat An official who represents his or her country in dealings with other countries.

draft To select individuals to be forced to serve in the military.

fusilier A member of certain regiments in the British Army.

neutrality A position of not taking sides in an argument or conflict.

no-man's land The space between two lines of opposing trenches.

parapet A protective wall of earth along the top of a trench.

periscope A long tube with mirrors that allows a submariner to see things on the surface of the ocean.

propaganda Material designed to make an audience think positively or negatively about a certain point of view.

ration A fixed amount of something, such as food or supplies, allowed to people in a time of shortage.

reparations Payments made to cover damages caused by a war.

salient A bulge that juts out of a straight line to form an angle.

stalemate A position in a contest in which neither side can win.

trench A long, narrow ditch.

U-boat An abbreviation for *Untersee-boote*, German for submarine.

ultimatum A demand to another country which, if it is not met, will lead to war.

FURTHER INFORMATION

Books

Fromwitz, Lori. *World War I and Modern America: 1890–1930.* The Story of the United States. Edina, MN: Abdo Publishing Company, 2014.

Kent, Zachary. *World War I: From the Lusitania to Versailles.* The United States at War. Berkeley Heights, NJ: Enslow Publishing Inc, 2011.

McNeese, Tim. *World War I and the Roaring Twenties.* Discovering U.S. History. New York, NY: Chelsea House Publishing, 2010.

Price, Sean. *Yanks in World War I; Americans in the Trenches.* American History through Primary Sources. Chicago, IL: Raintree Fusion, 2008.

Samuels, Charlie. *Timeline of World War I.* Americans at War. New York, NY: Gareth Stevens, 2011.

Saunders, Nicholas. *World War I: A Primary Source History.* In Their Own Words. New York, NY: Gareth Stevens Publishing, 2005.

Websites

www.pbs.org/greatwar
Extensive website to support the PBS documentary series *The Great War and the Shaping of the 20th Century.*

www.history.com/topics/world-war-i
History.com page with many videos about World War I.

www.digitalhistory.uh.edu
Click on "World War I" in the first column to access Digital History's resources for the period.

www.worldwar1.com
Widely recommended, privately-maintained website about all aspects of World War I.

Publisher's note to educators and parents: Our editors have carefully reviewed these websites to ensure that they are suitable for students. Many websites change frequently, however, and we cannot guarantee that a site's future contents will continue to meet our high standards of quality and educational value. Be advised that students should be closely supervised whenever they access the Internet.

INDEX